SHOOT ONLY AT THE RED AIRPLANE

Bill Coons

ISBN 978-1-4303-0715-0

Printed in the United States of America

SHOOT ONLY AT THE RED AIRPLANE

Contents

(This page intentionally left blank)

Forward

The Japanese attack on Pearl Harbor sent shock waves throughout the nation. It was a wake up call to the U.S. armed forces. The mighty Pacific Fleet stationed in Hawaii was decimated. Naval forces stationed in Hawaii were reduced to shambles. Military advisors were on call almost immediately to find out what went wrong, and more importantly, how to fix it. All options were explored to increase the effectiveness of the remaining operational ships.

A few top advisors suggested better methods of training for the anti-aircraft gunners aboard our ships. The existing systems of using kites, towed targets and others had proved woefully inadequate. For a gunner to learn how to destroy an enemy aircraft, a target was needed that would at least approximate the size and speed of an attacking aircraft.

The idea of radio controlled ("RC") target aircraft was not new but lay dormant for a decade as technology caught up sufficiently for it to be practical. Was this a time for resurrection?

This is the true story of the development of target aircraft drones from conception to successful deployment both during and after the war. You will see how these drones helped to train gunners to defend US ships against aerial attacks.

We will cover much of what happened from the very first RC drone up to and including 1952. We will describe a few drones considered for use, and pertinent specifications of drones that were actually purchased in quantity. We will also delve into the actual day to day activities of VU7-A, a squadron on the west coast and go along on three different target exercises in the Pacific to find out just how an exciting "no live pilot operator on board" ("NOLO") was carried out. To my knowledge, this will be the first time that pilots who were actually involved will be describing an authentic mission. You will experience the thrill of watching a real drone aircraft as it dives on a ship and tries to avoid the gunfire, while being controlled from another aircraft by radio control.

This book is not meant to be an all inclusive account of RC target drone history, but rather a compilation of responses to my own inquiries on the subject, and my personal recollections after having "been there, done that." The only quotes will be first hand. Any errors in names, places, or dates are unintentional.

I wish to thank certain individuals who contributed greatly to this book. Franklin Dailey, Victor Smith, Robert Gosnell, Lee DiNapoli, Debbie McBride, Reginald Denny Jr,. Ken Kiefer, Steve Hill, Bob Short, John Voss, Ted Heineman, Dan Nichleson, Peter Soule, Russell Naughton, Tom McPherson, Charlie Harris, Mark Hardin, and William Bayne, each of whom will be specifically noted in the following chapters. Thanks also to the many museums that have referred me to new sources or have contributed facts or material. Because the drone projects were considered top secret by the government and only recently declassified, there has been relatively little written on the subject of target aircraft. Hopefully, this book will shine some light on the existing darkness of the subject.

Chapter 1

Setting the Stage

Time 06:30 - AM Early 1946
Place: An old, seemingly abandoned air strip overlooking the Pacific Ocean.

A bright red U.S. Navy TD2C Culver Cadet has been circling for several minutes. It appears that he is looking for the landing site. The flaps are down and he turns into the downwind leg. It is apparent that he is going to land. He turns on final approach, lowers the gear and lands right on the runway. After slowing down, he makes a 180 degree turn and slowly taxis back to the departure end of the runway only to be met by a group of onlookers. He turns the aircraft into the wind and it looks like he is ready to take off again. But for some reason, the people are trying to hold the airplane back. To further add to the confusion he idles the engine and proceeds to climb out of the cockpit. This is getting a little out of hand.

The pilot walks back to the rear of the airplane to talk to the group. They seem startled as the engine in the Cadet starts to increase power and begins to roll down the runway. All efforts to stop the aircraft by trying to holding it back are met with a frustrating increase in speed. The Cadet is now just another headless horseman, roaring down the runway with no pilot on board.

Just about this time another aircraft appears on the downwind leg. It is a twin engine U.S. Navy JRB Beechcraft. He must have noticed the problems on the strip and has come to investigate. The bright red Cadet finally becomes airborne just as the JRB turns on final approach and is in hot pursuit. The twin is right on the tail of the unmanned fighter. He will probably follow it to see where it crashes and report the location.

At this point we will freeze the scenario. I promise to return later and complete the story.

This is an exciting and informative account that will expose possibly for the first time, an exercise that had a very dramatic effect on the outcome of WWII, but has been shrouded for many years in the area of confidential to top secret information.

Read on.

Chapter 2

The Story of Radio Control

The study of radio controlled ("RC") aircraft was not new. The project was approved and started back in 1917, but there was a conspicuous lack of success (and funding) of serious research and development until mid 1936. At that time, advances in aircraft design and electro-mechanical technology, especially in auto-pilot design, made it feasible to provide the fleet with a radio controlled target for use in anti-aircraft gunnery training. The size and speed of enemy aircraft could be simulated with it a sense of realism that towed targets could never achieve, and the resulting experience of much greater gunner effectiveness.

The original criteria called for a seaplane capable of at least 100 mph, strong enough to withstand a catapult launch under radio control, capable of performing all normal flight maneuvers, and controllable to a range of at least ten miles. It was to be able to take off, land, and simulate firing runs, all while operating from a ship at sea.

The Chief of Naval Operations, Adm. William H. Standley, USN, heartily approved the project and backed it up with a very favorable report after a visit to the Royal Navy where target aircraft had been in use for some time. Standley's report was severely criticized by the Bureau of Ordinance, which did not have room or facilities to take on the project, and therefore questioned the feasibility of such a project.

In July, Lt. Comdr. D. S. Fahrney, USN, was named Officer in Charge of the Radio Controlled Aircraft Project. His first priorities were to include a landplane in the RC specifications and to determine if an auto pilot would be necessary.

The first examples, now called drones, were ordered for later delivery. Work proceeded using other available aircraft, namely the TU-2 and the TG-2.

Early tests with the drones were not without problems. The engineering department made vast improvements on auto-pilot design and RC equipment, the autopilot was improved by linking it with a turn and bank instrument and the radios improved considerably. In 1937, a drone took off, control was successfully transferred to a controller aircraft, several maneuvers flown, runway alignment established, and control returned to the ground controller for a successful landing on three successive tests. This achievement placed the United States at the forefront of worldwide drone technology in 1937.

The aircraft that were used in earlier tests were surplus ones consigned from existing inventories for drone research, and were considered expendable. As many as several hundred at a time were made available. Progress continued in the field of electronics and radio control systems.

As another war was appearing more and more likely, it was obvious that flyable aircraft deemed "surplus" in peacetime would likely be recalled for many essential services until production could catch up with new needs. The Navy was well aware they needed drones of different types designed for different purposes. Target drones were needed for fleet gunnery training Some were actual guided missiles, and some would have to carry explosives for destroying bridges and submarine pens.

While the Navy worked to develop and deploy drones, the fleet could only rely on older forms of gunnery training. One of these was the aerial kite designed by Paul Garber, who worked for the Smithsonian at the beginning of WW2 and would later be one of the creators of the National Air & Space Museum. Not to be confused with a child's kite on the end of a piece of string, gunnery kites were used to simulate attacking aircraft when towed from the rear of a ship under way. Gunnery officers aboard ship had responsibility for this type of training.

Flown with two lines operating a wooden rudder, these were very maneuverable. Special schools trained operators to make them perform loops, dives, figure eights and zig-zags. The kite was five feet in size and weighed less than two pounds. A silhouette of an enemy plane was painted on the front and blue in the surrounding area, so that only the plane was prominent. The apparent size varied with the length of the cable and could approximate that of an attacking plane. Over time, a lot of work improved the kite's ability to simulate many aerial threats. Compared to other types of targets, its airplane like appearance, flexibility of movement, variable range, ability to linger in range, simplicity of operation and ease of construction and repair made it extremely cost effective.

Target sleeves towed initially by a seaplane were introduced in 1921. These were quickly standardized in size, being some 10 feet long and approximately 42 inches in diameter. The length of the tow cable was 2,500 to 5,500 feet and more depending on the situation. At best, the sleeves simulated an attacking aircraft on a horizontal bombing run. An initial test involving several battleships revealed the desperate need for such training, as guns malfunctioned and no hits were scored on the sleeve. All these gunners were graduates of the Navy's Gunnery School. At Gunnery School, students lined up ten in a row and took turns shooting at clay pigeons. Targets could come from several directions and different angles. To hit one, a student had to quickly approximate its trajectory and "lead" (aim in front of) it such that the target and the shot would arrive at the same place at the same time. Each student fired ten rounds and moved to the back of the line to await his turn again. The physical bruising on the arms and shoulders from the considerable kick of each shot limited trainee learning endurance on the range.

Students then progressed to an electrically operated turret with a single shotgun mounted in it and more clay pigeons. Once they became proficient with this, they trained with a .30 caliber machine gun and finally a .50 caliber one. Many hours were then spent in a simulator trying to hit movies of enemy aircraft attacking your position.

When its "graduate" gunners were unable to hit a target sleeve towed by an aircraft, the Navy immediately understood that additional training with aircraft towed target sleeves and live ammo was necessary.

The Navy SNJ aircraft was one of several selected to tow targets housed in a compartment under the aircraft at the end of a 1/8" steel cable. A sleeve operator occupied the back seat and used winches to deploy the sleeve, control the length of the cable, and retrieve it after practice. More that one tow plane pilot requested reassignment to other duties after his aircraft was accidentally hit by errant machine gun bullets. Nonetheless, towed sleeves became a necessary part of gunnery training.

Paul Garber's Aerial Kite used to train anti-aircraft gunners in WW2. Garber was one of the founders of the Air and Space Museum.

TBM Target-Towing Squadron VU-5 at Tachikawa Air Force Base in Japan. Courtesy: Victor Smith

Chapter 3

Intro to RC

In 1936, the Navy was committed to getting their drone program under way. They ordered 4 Stearman Hammond Y planes. This aircraft was designed with a very simple two control system. It could be steered on the ground with just the yoke, and no rudder input. On the floor was a flap control and a brake. It also featured a swing-over control column to allow either pilot to fly; but perhaps most important, it featured a tri-cycle landing gear. Although at this point no take-offs or landings had been attempted from the ground without a safety pilot on board, it was known that "conventional" landing gear presented unique and difficult ground handling challenges for radio control.

The Stearman Hammond had a 125 HP engine, pusher type propeller and twin boom rear fuselage with aluminum control surfaces. It had a 40 foot wingspan and weighed 1,200 lbs. Safety regulations required all drones be configured to carry a safety pilot. The Navy could not risk having run-away drones crash out of control in a populated area. This necessitated a drone with a full set of controls in the cockpit and a way to disengage the radio to give the pilot control in an emergency. The added expense was considerable, and would eventually become a limiting factor on drone acquisition and use.

To develop a radio control drone, Lt. Cmdr. Fahrney formed a unit called Project Dog. At a time when the ordinance group was claiming that they had no problems, and the pilots were insisting that they did, definitive and unbiased answers were needed.

Hammond could not deliver their aircraft on schedule, so the Navy started with two Curtiss Fledgling N2C-2 training planes. Later they would be modified to accept a tricycle gear. The radio gear was the GP-2 transmitter and the RV-3 receiver. The radio and automatic pilot systems had improved to achieve routine reliability. The radio was designed with twelve channels. Elevator, aileron, and throttle, used two channels each, leaving several channels for future options.

Most control aircraft were the single engine Great Lakes TG-2 biplanes with 3 seats. The seat facing forward carried the controller and afforded a good view to keep the drone in sight. Tests were made using a radio control station mounted on a cart to experiment with ground control.

A 1930 New Standard NT-1 training plane had radio controls installed and was to be used as a drone. It was a test vehicle for making sure that all electronics and control systems worked. It was never flown without a safety pilot.

In March 1937 a test flight was conducted using a TG-2 control plane and the NT drone. A safety pilot was on board and both planes were in the air. A check without using the radio proved fine when the radio was disconnected, but when a right turn was attempted by radio control, the plane turned left. The safety pilot took over and landed the airplane. The controls had been crossed, which was easy to fix, and further tests were successful.

In November 1937, 4 complete takeoffs and landings were made under radio control with a safety pilot. Later that same day, the drone was successfully taken off from a ground station without a safety pilot, control was passed to a control plane, and several maneuvers carried out. After aligning the control plane with the runway, the control plane passed control back to the ground station for landing. An unfortunate bad landing left the drone in poor shape, but the overall success of the flight without a safety pilot aboard greatly improved the credibility of the overall program.

In December 1937, the Stearman Hammond Y planes were delivered. One was configured as a drone, and tests were carried out with no pilot aboard and completed as planned. The tests with the JH were considered Top Secret, with information little and hard to come by. We do know that in August 1938, the USS Ranger became the first ship to use the drones for target practice, and the target drone was never hit. The next month the USS Utah scored several direct hits and the drone was destroyed.

Following these exercises, a study examined the feasibility of using television with a camera/transmitter in the drones and a receiver in the control planes. If one could guide a drone from another aircraft by watching a screen, it would be a giant step toward guided missile capability.

In 1940 and 1941, several aircraft were tested and used as drones. New technology in the radio transmitter used a modulator to send a signal along with the carrier to separate the channels. After the receiver in the drone received the signal, the signal was sent to a selector that sorted out the command, and then to a relay box. The relay box then converted it to a small voltage output which in turn opened or closed a relay. This provided the voltage to operate the hydraulic servos. The transmitter box had many controls. On the top right side was a stick about 5 inches long that would move in four directions. Pushing forward gave down elevator. Back was up elevator. Left was left aileron, and by moving the stick to the right gave right aileron. It was similar to transmitter boxes for radio controlled model airplanes.

On the left side of the box there were two switches. On the left was a "stepper switch" with "up" positions ranging from one through ten available for controlling the functioning of throttle, brakes, flaps, landing gear, and so on by toggling it up. Toggling it "down" once would reset it to zero. On the right was another switch with which to select "yes" or "no" functions and increments in between the extremes. To take the drone off from a runway, one would move the left "stepper switch" to position one to select the throttle. By toggling the right "switch" up, one would advance to maximum throttle. By toggling it down, back power was reduced as necessary.

To retract the landing gear after take off, you would reset the stepper switch by pressing down once and then "up" three times to select the landing gear function. With the right hand switch you could then raise (or lower) the gear, pressing "up" to raise the gear and "down" to lower it. It sounds difficult, but with practice it became second nature. With control of the rudder, centering switch, and throttle cut off, the full range of drone control was available. Control box designs varied somewhat because of constant and incremental improvements.

That is what the radios could do from the outside. Here is what was going on inside.

Much has been written about the names, models, and serial numbers of radios used in target aircraft drones, but very little has been written about how they actually worked.

Most of the radios used before and during WW2 were not complicated. It seems so when you think that by moving a joy stick on a control box to the left, would cause a drone to turn to the left. Here is how it worked:

The drone controller aircraft has a control box, a transmitter, and a modulator. That is all that is necessary to send a signal to the drone. The drone has a receiver, a selector and a relay box. On the control box is a joy stick for elevator and rudder (sometimes ailerons), plus an assortment of switches for throttle, brakes, flaps etc. Each one of these functions is assigned a separate audio frequency.

The transmitter sends out a constant carrier frequency. As the carrier signal passes through the modulator, it picks up the audio signal and sends it along with the carrier. The carrier and the tone are on their way.

When the signal reaches the drone, it is picked up by the receiver and is sent directly to the selector. The selector sorts out the selected audio tone and sends it to a bank of reeds. The reeds are small and flexible. They will vibrate when it hears a certain frequency. It will only recognize that particular audio tone. You may have as many reeds as you need as long as you have enough audio tones available.

When the reed detects the correct tone it will begin to vibrate. The tips of the reed will fluctuate enough to make contact with a relay. Each reed and relay combination is assigned a circuit that turns on a servo motor that operates that assigned function.

In simple terms, it goes like this. For left rudder: Push the stick on the control box to the left, the modulator picks the rudder tone and sends it out with the carrier frequency. The receiver in the drone selects the signal, sends it to the selector and the reed that is tuned to the signal starts to vibrate and turns the rudder relay on. The servo turns on and is connected to a pushrod that turns the rudder to the left.

As you can see, it is not that complicated and much of the success of such radios was related to simplicity. The problem with the radio was that it used vacuum tubes,and lots of them. The tubes were prone to vibration, blowing out, and simply wearing out. They had to be checked continuously. The transmitters could contain up to 30 tubes and the only way to check them was to use a tube checker, often.

Ironically, even though the transistor was invented in 1946, the military continued using tubes well into the 1950s.

Chapter 4

1939-1940

Up to this point, aircraft used in the drone program were existing older designs deemed "surplus" to current requirements. As advances in radios and auto pilot designs exceeded the limited performance of these older planes, thought was given to the design requirements for a target drone that was more nimble and could be mass produced should the need arise. Surplus aircraft could be put back into service, or salvaged for useful parts. Anti-aircraft gunnery training requirements now demanded more reliable and nimble drones to raise proficiency to the highest possible level short of personal combat experience.

Events in Europe were as unsettling as they were unclear, and Congress was increasingly aware of the need to prepare for any possible eventuality, including all-out war.

On September 1st, 1939, Poland was invaded by Germany. Polish armies were crushed by the Nazi Blitzkrieg, and two days later, Britain and France declared war on Germany. On October 9, Hitler decided that he wanted to control everything in the west. The Soviets also attacked Poland. For six months, during what became known as the "Phony War", there was much posturing and little fighting.

On April 9, Norway and Denmark were invaded by Germany. Three weeks later it was France's turn. And on, and on, it went. The United States would remain officially neutral for awhile, at least on paper, even as other countries rushed to choose the side they would fight on in World War II.

Meanwhile, those at the drawing boards trying to design the ultimate aircraft drone adaptable for multiple uses, got a reprieve in that one was already in existence. While not exactly the ultimate design, it was small, maneuverable, fast, had simple three channel operation, and perhaps best of all, it was cheap and easy to produce in numbers.

What follows is the story of Reginald Denny's involvement in the development of RC drones. Mr. Denny's son, Reginald Denny, Jr., provided personal insight and photos for this book.

Reginald Denny, a British movie actor, came to America to further his career in the film industry, and played lead roles in many Hollywood films. As a hobby he designed, built and flew gasoline and rubber band powered free flight model airplanes with associates.

As a result of the friendship between their respective wives, both at Universal Studios in the late twenties, Denny met the heir to the Whittier Company millions. Becoming the best of friends, Paul Whittier arranged for the Whittier Company to finance Reginald Denny Industries. They opened a model airplane shop on Hollywood Boulevard in 1935.

By 1938 personal circumstances forced Reginald Denny to file bankruptcy. At this point, Reginald Denny Industries was spending more money than it was making, and the Whittier Company was looking for a way, any way, to get out.

Kenneth Case, a very knowledgeable and talented radio ham, was probably the source of their idea of remotely controlling a model by radio signals. He joined Reginald Denny Industries in late '38 or early '39, and played a major role in development of radio controlled models. Their first effort was relatively large (for a model) and clearly underpowered.

In 1939 the Whittier Company leased RDI to Peter Veer. He was to form a new company, Radioplane, to further develop and attempt to commercially produce radio-controlled model "drones." Denny was very enthusiastic about Radioplane but, being personally of limited funds, was forced to seek venture capital if the project was to proceed.

A banker friend, Bill Neary, introduced him to Whit Collins and Harold Powell of the Elastic Stop Nut Company. Radioplane became owned 50% by Collins/Powell and 25% each to Denny and Whittier. Powell became President, Denny became Vice President, and the rest of the Board included Whitley Collins, William Larrabee and Ferris Smith.

They contracted with Righter Manufacturing, of Burbank, CA, to assist with final design and building of the prototype drone. Walt Righter and his company designed and built all the engines for all of the Radioplanes.

Initially, Reginald Denny handled most sales and Public Relations duties for Radioplane. In late '39 or early '40, Denny, Righter and Case demonstrated various Radioplanes to the Army and secured a military contract for the RP-4. Two hangars were leased at Van Nuys

Airport for production of the"OQ-1." The designation "OQ" was the Army's identification prefix for "subscale target." At some point, Powell and Collins (with Denny's OK) convinced Whittier to sell them his 25% share of Radioplane for an undisclosed amount of money.

When the Navy became interested and designated their version "TDD-1" or Target Drone Denny, Powell and Collins reassigned Denny to be in charge of plant maintenance. From that time on he was excluded from meaningful involvement in company management.

Board member, Ferris Smith, was an aeronautical engineer at Lockheed hired by Whit Collins to be Chief Engineer, a function previously performed by Walt Righter from his Burbank company. His real professional involvement probably came in 1941, when full production was started. Between the Army and Navy, 14,891 OQ-2 drones were produced. The later TDD-2 model with a Righter 0-15-3 engine could do 102 mph. The TDD-3 with a Righter/Kiekhaefer 0-45-1 22 HP engine could reach a speed of 140 mph.

In 1948 Denny requested a short leave of absence from Radioplane to play a part in the film, "Mr. Blandings Builds His Dream House", with James Stewart. His request was refused and he was told he would be terminated if he left to take the part.

Denny did take the part and was terminated from Radioplane, with no knowledge of discussions between Powell, Collins and Jack Northrup about merging Radioplane with Northrup Aviation. Dejected (and without continuing income), Denny sold his 25% share of Radioplane to Powell and Collins for a one-time payment of $60,000. He was never again involved with aircraft, model or otherwise. Upon his separation from Radioplane Inc. in 1948, he went on to further pursue his acting career.

Returning to England in his retirement, Denny died there penniless in 1967. Radioplane did merge with Northrup and Collins, one of Denny's original investment partners, soon became President there but that's another story.

Reginald Denny's contribution to drone development and use was both unique and significant. As the individual primarily responsible for moving the drone idea from dreams to reality, he is considered the "father" of target aircraft drones.

Walter Righter's involvement in the TDD series has earned him a place in history for the design and manufacture of engines that powered the TDD Radioplane drone series.

For two years, Navy Lt. JG Lee Di Napoli operated the target drones named after Denny – the TDD's - from a US Navy AVR boat out of Santa Ana, CA. Mr. Di Napoli added these interesting facts.

Di Napoli's AVR drone control boat was 63 feet long. Its two 16 cylinder Hall-Scott gasoline engines burned aviation fuel and gave it a top speed of about 40 knots. A catapult in the front of the boat launched the drones.

The drone operation was attached to the VU-8 Utility squadron based at Santa Ana called a KD unit. It consisted of one junior officer, a CPO, a radioman, an aviation mechanic, a metal smith and three seamen. Their original base of operations was from the city dock at Newport Beach, but later they moved to the Naval ammunition depot at Seal Beach.

As stated earlier, the TDD drone was manufactured by the Radioplane Company founded by Reginald Denny (which was later acquired by Northrop Corp). The TDD was basically a huge radio controlled model airplane approximately 8 feet long with a wingspan of 12 feet 3 inches. The fuselage was constructed of steel tubing and covered with canvas.

The engine was manufactured by McCullough Motors, today better known for their gasoline chain saws and line trimmers. The engine was 2-cycle with two opposed cylinders rated at 40 HP. The throttle was not controllable, so the engine was preset to 3550 rpm before launch for each flight which was limited by fuel to one hour. Two radio channels operated the elevator and rudder controls. Another sent a signal to energize a solenoid to open a hinged cover and deploy a parachute to bring the drone down without damage. This parachute compartment was in the upper part of the fuselage.

Shipboard anti-aircraft gunnery practice using the drones was scheduled by the Navy gunnery command in San Diego, and schedules were posted a week in advance. The Navy divided the ocean between San Clemente and Catalina islands into five mile grids. For example, the Monday morning schedule might call for the AVR to rendezvous with a destroyer squadron at 0800 in grid G-5 and later with a carrier at 1200 in grid J-7. Although they had 3 boats, only one AVR was used for a mission, which could last from an hour to an hour and a half. The ships were not notified in advance of the types of runs they would encounter. For simulated strafing runs the drone would be in a shallow dive from about 1500 feet toward the ship, jinking left and right to simulate the evasive action possible by an enemy pilot. Torpedo runs were flown at a steady altitude of about 150 feet.

Rigid safety rules greatly limited accidents. Over a three year span, only once did a drone actually strike a ship. In that instance, the drone was hit while simulating a strafing run on a ship. It was on fire, and control of elevator, rudder and parachute were all lost. The engine kept running and the drone continued the established dive toward the ship. All the AVR boat could do was to notify the ship to have personnel take cover. Some antenna wires strung between two masts took the "hit" and the drone dropped to the deck. No one was hurt and there was little damage to the ship.

Drone reliability was very high, around 90 percent. Most mishaps occurred during launching operations. Engine torque tended to roll the drone to the left off the catapult. Even immediate application of right rudder could be ineffective to counter the effect of propeller torque and high gusty winds, and a drone could snap roll in. The engines and radios were very reliable, and problems with them were very rare.

The AVR boats trained destroyer, carrier, battleship, cruiser, sub, transport, and communication ship gunners. A KD unit went aboard for exercises, as ships did not have their own radio controls. The drones were flown much the same as aircraft RC models. Controllers with only a choice of up, down, left, and right control inputs had a constant challenge to distinguish left turns from right ones from a distance. They had to mentally put themselves in the cockpit of the drone, because the necessary control input had to be reversed when the drone was coming toward them.

The school for drone controllers and crews was at NAS Santa Ana. When Lt. DiNapoli was there, training took about three months. After a week in the classroom, students went to a large open field near Lake Irvine for hands-on drone instruction and experience. An instructor would launch the drone and take it up to about 1000 feet. The student would then take over and get the "feel" of left and right turns, coming and going, climbing, diving and recovering from unusual attitudes.

When students had enough experience and confidence, they would tackle and master the less forgiving launch procedures.

As each controller student qualified and was graduated, he would get orders to a KD unit to replace another officer due to be relieved. Crews sent to the school learned to maintain and repair drone radios, airframe, engines, etc. Some seamen were trained to pack the parachute. Once training was complete, the boat and its crew were ready to operate independently as a fully contained unit.

US Navy 63 ft. AVR Boat used by the Navy to catapult TD drones by radio control and use them for anti-aircraft practice. Photo Courtesy: Lee DiNapoli.

Reginald Denny's Model Shop in Hollywood, CA (It all started here!) North America's first successful mass-produced target drone program. Photo by Pete Soule.

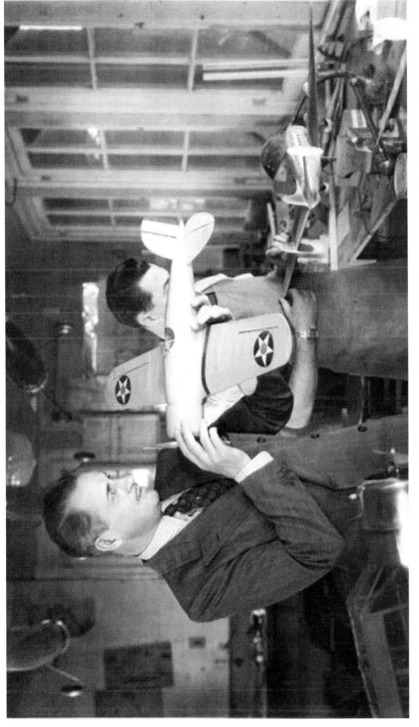

Reginald Denny in his workshop inspecting a model. Courtesy: Reginald Denny Jr.

Walter Righter's engine plant. They produced twin and four cylinder engines for the drones until 1946. Some in 1946.
http//www.ctie.monash.edu.au/hargrave/dernny.html

OQ-14 on its test stand.
http//www.ctie.monash.edu.au/hargrave/dernny.html

Righter's twin opposed cylinders for the RP-4. Luca Mariotti relates: Accepted in May 1939. One of 53 drone engines produced for the army. Courtesy of: www.ctie.monash.edu.au/hargrove.denny.html

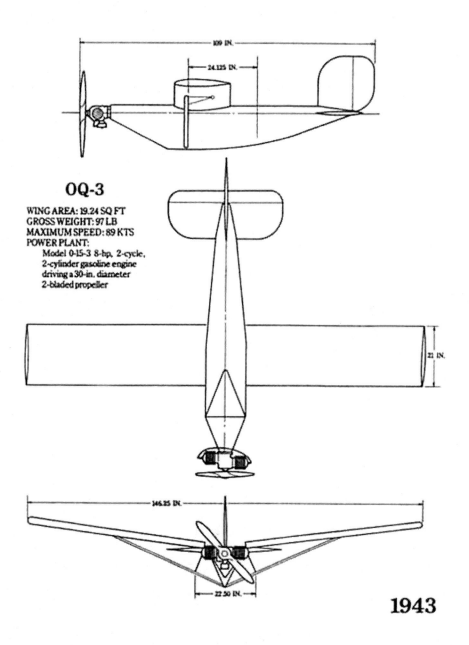

OQ-3

WING AREA: 19.24 SQ FT
GROSS WEIGHT: 97 LB
MAXIMUM SPEED: 89 KTS
POWER PLANT:
  Model 0-15-3 8-hp, 2-cycle,
  2-cylinder gasoline engine
  driving a 30-in. diameter
  2-bladed propeller

1943

OQ-3 # view
http//www.ctie.monash.edu.au/hargrave/dernny.html

1937 Denny Ad. Courtesy of: www.ctie.monash.edu.au/hargrave/denny.html

Aviation Movie Photo Op. Courtesy of: Reginald Denny Jr.

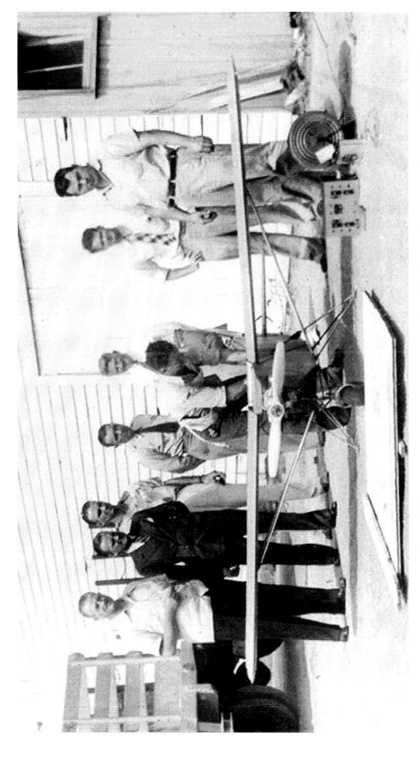

Righter Test Group. Left to right: R. Denny, unknown, Paul Whittier, unknown, unknown, Al DeLisle bending over model, Ken Case, Walter Righter. Courtesy of: www.ctie.monash.edu.au/hargrove.denny.html

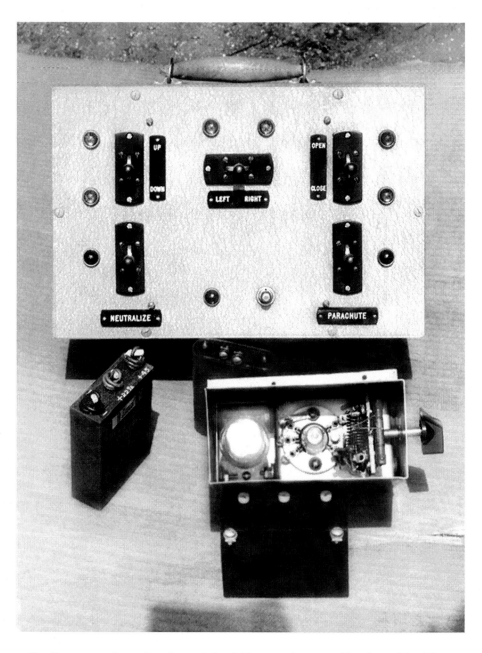

Radio transmitter for the original Denny drones. Designed by Ken Case. http//www.ctie.monash.edu.au/hargrave/denny.html

Preparing the drone for launch aboard USS New York.
Photo by Capt. T.C. Edrimgton 111.

An aviation radio crew checking a drone after it had been recovered from an anti-aircraft gunnery exercise aboard ship. The drone had survived the flight and the parachute had deployed to allow recovery. All sorts of little problems had to be addressed because chances were that it had been hit by gunfire somewhere. These drones always seemed to gather interest on the deck.

Courtesy of www.ctie.monash.edu.au/hargrave/denny.html

A TDD catapults from the deck of USS New York in 1943. The drone will be guided through a series of gunnery training exercises. It will be recovered by deploying a built in parachute.
Photo by Capt. T.C. Edrington 111.

OOPS... This was a drone demonstration for the Army. Something went wrong. They were awarded the contract anyway. http//www.ctie.monash.edu.au/hargrave/denny.html

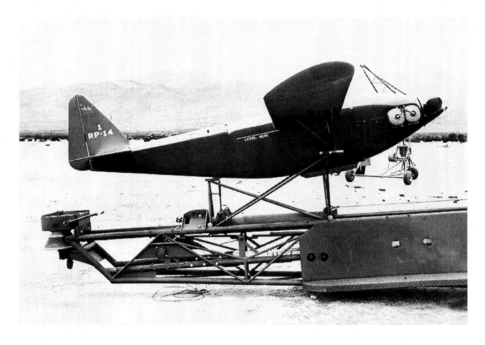

RP-14 "Jake" OQ-14 on the catapult 1944. More powerful 22 HP 168 MPH with Righter O-45, 4 cylinder engine http//www.ctie.monash.edu.au/hargrave/denny.html.

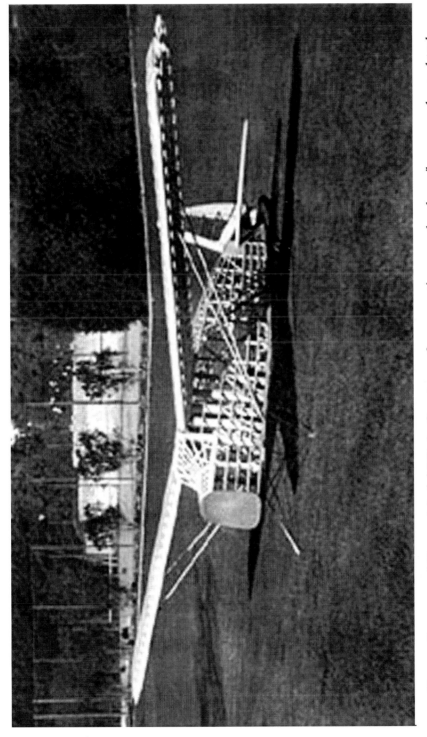

Photo of uncovered Denny Model RP-4. Courtesy of: www.ctie.monash.edu.au/hargrove.denny.html

Drone Destroyed.
Permission: www.ctie.monash.edu.au/hargrove.denny.html

TDD Saved by parachute.
The chute deploys when when the drone runs out of fuel.
Permission: www.ctie.monash.edu.au/hargrove.denny.html

Catapult launch of Radioplane OQ-2A. Photo by: Luca Mariotti

37

RP-4/OQ-1 Radioplanes awaiting testing at Muroc Dry Lake 1939.
Courtesy of: www.ctie.monash.edu.au/hargrave/denny.htm

Shockcord Catapult used on AVR boats for very short takeoffs.
Courtesy of: www.ctie.monash.edu.au/hargrave/denny.htm

OQ-3. Parachute hatch opens automatically when the drone runs out of fuel. http//www.ctie.monash.edu.au/hargrave/denny.html

TDD testing group. Whitley Collins, Harold Powell, Al DeLisle, Ken Case, Reg. Denny, Paul Whitley, unknown. http//www.ctie.monash.edu.au/hargrave/denny.html

Reginald Denny and his Dennymite. Courtesy of: Reginald Denny Jr.

This is not a launch. It is actually conducting a wind-tunnel test. Courtesy of: www.ctie.monash.edu.au/hargrave/denny.htm

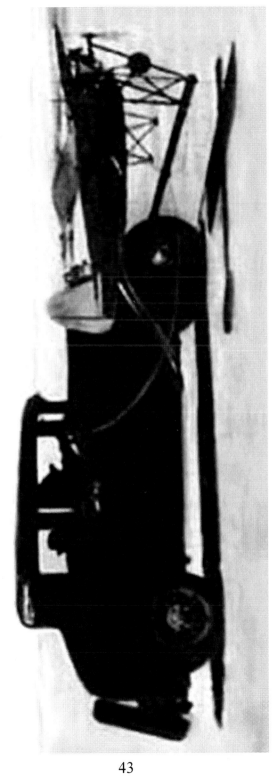

A portable wind tunnel mounted on the front of a car checks the aerodynamics of the drone.
Courtesy of: www.ctie.monash.edu.au/hargrave/denny.htm

Actor Robert Montgomery and his personalized Denny plane. Courtesy of: Reginald Denny Jr.

44

Reginald Denny and Walter Righter with RP-1. Courtesy of: Reginald Denny Jr.

45

Chapter 5

TDR-1

With the target drone project doing well, thoughts turned to the possibility of assault drones utilizing the new proximity fuse and the improvements in radar and television.

Before the proximity fuse was invented, the detonation was by direct contact, a timer set at launch, or a barometric fuse sensing a preset altitude. With a proximity fuse, all that was necessary was to get the shell on a path that would determine when it was close enough to the target to destroy it. Radio waves reflected by the target determined the distance using the Doppler Effect to compare the incoming waves. As an example, the difference in the sound of a train whistle as it passes. Leading the target was still necessary because the closer a shell exploded to the target, the more damage would be inflicted.

Improved radar could now detect objects on a horizontal plane and look ahead, and a radar altimeter that could provide an accurate altitude. Lt. Cmdr. Fahrney recommended designing a drone that would include these additions to deliver a bomb or torpedo.

The Radio Corporation of America and its engineers started working on a television system to enable the drone to send pictures back to a drone controller or ground station of what the drone could see. Specifications included an interference free radio control, radio altimeter, auto pilot, and a television camera and receiver. This greatly increased the weight of the drone's electronics gear.

Successful simulated torpedo attacks were made by the television and proved successful even though the drone was never in visual contact with the controller. The Chief of Bureau of Aeronautics then proposed the use of obsolete SBDs, and SB2Cs, since these aircraft would be heavier, faster, and be able to carry the heavier electronics package.

It was obvious that any proposed drone design needed to be manufactured by companies without other military contracts. The military had enough on their minds with war production without worrying about a drone that was not yet proven in combat. Major components and a majority of hardware should be stock items readily available due to the existing high priority.

After December 7, 1941, the Navy needed every flyable aircraft in its inventory for combat training. Obsolete SBDs and SB2Cs were withdrawn from the drone program even as the highest priority was assigned to the design of an assault drone.

Capt. Oscar Smith, USN was assigned as Director of Plans Division of the Chief of Naval Operations drone project. He stated the United States "didn't need a suicide pilot" to attack an enemy ship with an unmanned radio controlled drone fitted with a television camera and transmitter. He wanted controller aircraft capable of controlling a drone from take off to the target even if the visual contact between the drone and controller was lost. He wanted a bomb or torpedo with an automatic homing device to be carried by the drone and automatically released when a successful hit was most likely.

The Bureau of Aeronautics was directed to produce 200 expendable assault drones, and the Naval Aircraft Factory was ordered to manufacture 100 designated as the TDN-1.

Specifications:

Construction	Plywood
Wing span	48 feet
Weight	3900 lbs.
Speed	140 mph
Range	140 miles
Engines	2- 0-435, 220 HP. Stock
Warhead	2000 lb bomb or torpedo.

The Interstate Aircraft and Engineering Company designed the drones. With its years of aviation construction experience, it was the logical choice to manufacture them. The Navy purchased the Arlington Furniture Company, which boasted the longest furniture production line in the country, for lease to Interstate. In September, 1942, following a tour of their facility in De Kalb, IL, the Rudolph Wurlitzer Corp. was selected as a major subcontractor because their workers were highly skilled with long experience in making wood products.

Re-designated the TDR-1, the drones were of compressed and molded plywood construction, and their cockpit could accommodate a safety pilot. During, and especially over populated areas, a pilot was always aboard in case of an emergency. Its long spindly landing gear made it look somewhat like a preying mantis. This gear was designed to be jettisoned after take off on a one way flight carrying a bomb or torpedo.

A Grumman TBF with special equipment installed and a crew of four controlled the drone. The control pilot (CPP) sat in the front seat. The drone control pilot (DCP) sat in the rear seat. Two radiomen sat in the bilge and operated the electronics. The CCP would guide the drone to an area near the target, transfer control to the DCP and turn away from the target to be clear of enemy fire. The DCP would confirm control of the drone and guide it to hit the target using a "forward view" image transmitted from the camera in the drone to the small television screen in front of him. Civilians first saw similar images on television transmitted by "smart bombs" used almost 50 years later during the Gulf War.

After the surprise attack on Pearl Harbor but before the battle of Midway, Admiral King pushed for rapid procurement and use of the assault drone. Employed soon and in sufficient numbers, such a weapon would enjoy the battlefield advantage of surprise until effective countermeasures could be developed and employed by the Japanese. Unfortunately, the development of the idea took years.

The Radio Corporation of America came up with a radar homing system called a "SNIFFER." Operating in a horizontal plane, this could release a torpedo or bomb a predetermined distance from a target and correct its trajectory left or right until impact. In April of 1943, a drone locked onto a tanker 2 miles away. It was the first successful radar homing test on a moving target in the war. Within the year good results were possible at speeds from 90 to 180 knots within a 4 mile radius of such a drone.

By 1944, the situation in the Pacific had improved. Admiral Nimitz believed our conventional weapons again capable of winning the war, and recommended that SBDs be used as drones as they became available. These were faster and more maneuverable than the drones then in use, and they could easily carry the additional weight of increasingly sophisticated electronics gear with significantly more explosives.

On March 10, 1944, a directive reduced the number of assault drones to 338. Electronics procurement was not reduced because the excess could be installed in obsolete planes. The United States now had a fully operational and reliable remote control explosive delivery system of proven capability in actual combat.

On September 5,1944, Commander Robert F. Jones was chosen to head up a special air task force called Stag One. The operation was so "top secret" that some details of its operation were not declassified until July, 1979. On September 22nd 1944, 46 TDR drones departed the Sterling and Green Islands area for targets in the Shortland and Rabul areas. All took off successfully. Two were lost in route to the target area due to radio signal interference. Seven others were lost due to other malfunctions. The remaining 37 launched attacks. Three were downed by the enemy before reaching their targets. Five were lost due to television malfunctions, and the remaining twenty six attacks are believed to have hit their intended targets.

On October 20, 1944, a controller guided TDR destroyed a Japanese freighter. A few days later the drones were used to attack Japanese anti-aircraft positions on Ballale and Peperang Islands with disappointing results. Some were lost in route and some were shot down.

On December 12th, 1944, for reasons now not entirely clear, the TDR special task force was abruptly discontinued.

Interstate TDR-1. Photograph courtesy of: National Museum of Naval Aviation

51

TDR-1 with cockpit removed. Photograph courtesy of: National Museum of Naval Aviation

XTDR-1 used in the Pacific. Photograph courtesy of: National Museum of Naval Aviation

XTDR-1 withcockpit. Photograph courtesy of: National Museum of Naval Aviation

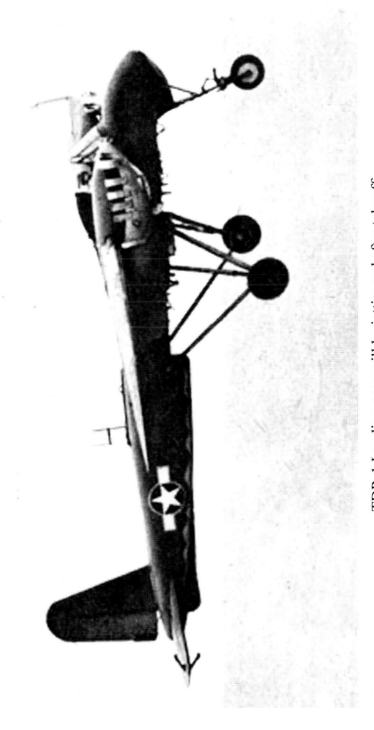

TDR-1 Landing gear will be jettisoned after takeoff.
Photograph courtesy of: National Museum of Naval Aviation

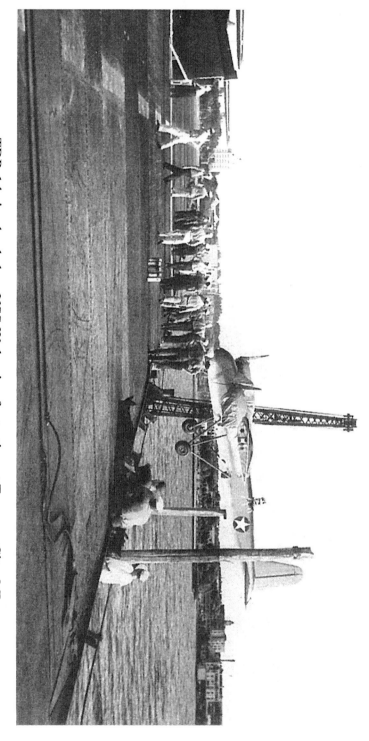

TDR-1 being loaded on USS Wolverine for testing at Traverse City, MI. Photograph courtesy National Archive.

Interstate TDR-1 drone, flying with a safety pilot. This version was manufactured in De Kalb, and in Lewis Lockport, IL.. It was considered top secret at the time. Factory employees were required to sign a secrecy agreement. The Army version operated with a landing gear, which was jettisoned after take off, but the Navy version was launched by a catapult. Photograph courtesy of National Museum of Naval Aviation

TDR3-1. Photograph courtesy of: National Museum of Naval Aviation

Chapter 6

PQ-14 (TD2C)

In August of 1940, the Army Air Force was directed to procure a new breed of target aircraft to complement the TDD Dennyplane. It would have to be faster and capable of carrying a ferry pilot. Not to be confused with using TDRs carrying explosives on a one way trip to the enemy, following NOLO (acronym for No Live Pilot Operator) gunnery exercises these drones were expected to normally return without significant damage for re-use. They would need to reliably land under remote control again and again.

Twenty aircraft companies were invited to bid. Culver, located in Columbus, Ohio, became the only company to supply the Army and Navy such drones in quantity during the war.

The 90hp PQ-8 was based on the Culver Model LFA Cadet sport plane. This small, fast, retractable landing gear ship was very maneuverable, and already in mass production. Its fuselage, wings, etc. being stressed plywood skins, saved aluminum and offered a challenge to enemy radar. The subsequent PQ-8A was even faster.

The PQ-14 was perhaps the pinnacle of the design. No less than 2,043 PQ-14s were produced during WW2 with 1,198 going to the Navy (designated as TD2Cs). The PQ-14 could challenge fighter pilots and B-29 gunners at altitudes up to 17,000 feet in addition to realistic Kamikaze-style "attacks" for shipboard anti-aircraft practice.

PQ-14 Specs.:

> Type man Carrying Aerial Target
> Crew 1
> Engine 150 HP Franklin O-300-11
> Wing span 30 ft.
> Length 19 ft. 6 inches.
> Height 8 ft. 4-1/2 inches
> Maximum speed 180 MPH
> Ferry range 594 miles
> Service ceiling 17,000 ft.
> Armament none

They were typically controlled from Twin Beechcraft JRB-1s. Those produced with a glazed nose to give the controller a greater view were called "Expeditors."

Following are notes from Bob Short, Culver Aircraft 1942-1946 –

Al Mooney's Culver Dart was probably the basic design from which improvements ultimately yielded the entire PQ series. Only forty five were produced. The Culver Cadet was completed and first flown in December 1939. The little two place (side by side) low wing monoplane with retractable landing gear and a Continental 75 horsepower engine was an immediate success.

Col. Holloman, from Wright Field, became interested in the Cadet as a drone to be flown either by a pilot or by radio control. He told Al Mooney if this was feasible he would sign a contract for 75 aircraft. That Army contract started Culver in the drone business. The Franklin Engine Co. was chosen to supply their 90hp flat four engine, and work began on installation of a remote radio control system for what would become the PQ-8. PQ was the military designation for "Man Carrying Aerial Target." Soon the Army wanted greater performance. The PQ-8A had a 125hp Lycoming engine. The Navy ordered 200 designated TDC (Target Drone Culver). By late 1941 radar directed anti-aircraft gun crews were getting much better at finding and tracking targets, and a contract was received for a drone that could operate at higher altitudes with a top speed of 190 mph. The new design, with a higher aspect wing ratio and a Franklin 155hp flat six engine was designated the PQ-9.

The prototype was completed in early 1942 and easily met the new speed requirement, but it was also necessary to demonstrate recovery from a high altitude 6 turn spin. The initial test resulted in the loss of the aircraft. It was at this point that Bob Short got into the picture. The tail arm was lengthened which improved directional stability.

The Army PQ-14 and Navy TD2C were the same airplane but each had different radio control equipment. The radios were made by different companies although some of the parts were interchangeable. The Army's PQ-14 had a whip antenna on the fuselage top half of the cockpit. The TD2C-1 had the same with the addition of a wire antenna from each wing tip to the top of the vertical tail fin. This was one way to determine whether the plane was a PQ-14 or a TD2C-1.

The aircraft was made of molded plywood which had to be waterproofed by the application of a sealer. Applying the sealer by brush took forever and production was greatly speeded up by building vats large enough to accommodate a fully assembled wing. A superior job now took only the time necessary for sealer in vats to penetrate a submerged structure.

Bob relates that a few PQ-14s were combat tested in the attack role. Some were loaded with explosives to flush out Japanese concealed in caves and tunnels. A few hundred pounds of high explosives was jammed into the cockpit and the drone was then guided by radio control into the tunnel entrance. The army had plans to establish a drone base at Guadalcanal for cave busting operations but when the A-bomb dropped, so did those plans.

Drone activity did not end with the war. U.S. Navy utility training squadrons based near the Pacific remained active, and anti-aircraft drone training was still going on into 1947 with Grumman F6F 5Ks.

On July 4th, 1946, Bob Short, a key man in the target drone arena, resigned from Culver. July 15th was his last day on the job.

The Navy TD2C was popular with ferry pilots because it was great fun to fly. So much so, in fact, that the elevator travel was later reduced (to keep hot rod pilots out of trouble) which tamed it down considerably. It became a veritable workhouse during and after the war. More than a few thought it was a shame to consign such a beautiful little sport plane to a program of probable destruction. Even crew members who were not pilots enjoyed just sitting in the cockpit during run-ups and performing radio checks.

PQ-13 Ercoupe

The following is information from William R. Bayne, Director Texas Ercoupe Museum, aviation historian and author.

Two of 112 prewar Ercoupes produced were purchased by the Army and designated PQ-13, one of two military designations given the standard civilian Engineering and Research Corporation (ERCO) design.

These monocoque metal monoplanes were powered by a Continental A-65 opposed four cylinder engine of 65hp and a Sensenich wooden propeller. They were 20 feet two inches in length with thirty foot wing spans. The design was uniquely well suited to remote control.

The tricycle-gear made the plane much easier to handle than one with "conventional" gear, and was designed to absorb a vertical landing impact of 15 feet per second! It was not, however, retractable; and the penalty for this was approximately 15 mph. The main gear had cast aluminum alloy main members fitted with oleo shock struts, rubber compression elements, hydraulic brakes and 7.00 x 4 tires. The nose gear was comprised of an oleo strut, taxi spring and a double-fork support for the 5.00 x 4 two-bearing wheel and tire.

The wings were set at 1-1/2° incidence to the horizontal stabilizer, each having 7° of dihedral. No flaps were necessary. An engine thrust line angled 3-1/2° down and 5° to the right resulted in minimal trim change from full power to gliding flight. Scale models proved the design inherently stable without a pilot.

Huge ailerons were aerodynamically balanced, and operated differentially with a maximum range of 20° up and 10° down such that, at maximum wheel deflection the up aileron would rise to 50° while the down aileron returned to about 7° below neutral. Twin rudders (which moved 20° outward but only 3° inward) could be interlinked to operate with aileron input (two-control) or in the normal manner (three-control). Elevator movement was limited to 13° up.

The result was a plane that could not stall (in the conventional sense) and that had actually been certified for production as "Incapable of Spinning" at a time in aviation history when the stall-spin crash was a leading cause of aviation fatalities.

The first PQ-13, AAF Serial No. 41-25196, was procured under Contract 41-1890 approved 9/20/40. It was manufactured 12/04/40 and purchased 1/4/41. This aircraft had a 1175 lb. gross weight, an empty weight of 733 lbs., and a useable load of 442 lbs. It carried a total of 14 gallons of fuel, with 9 gallons in a tank in the left wing and 5 gallons in a header tank mounted high in the fuselage between the firewall and the instrument panel. Its military Aircraft Record Card is so inaccurate as to appear fabricated, inasmuch as it is absolutely verifiable from other contemporary official records that it was NOT "received" on 12/8/41, and was NOT removed from flying status with only 2.8 flying hours since new. It does, however, appear that on or about 5/4/42 it was transferred as an instructional (non-flying) airframe to the Army Air Corps Technical School at Chanute Field near Champaign, Illinois.

The second, AAF Serial No. 41-39099, was procured under Contract W-535 ac15093. It was manufactured 8/13/41 and purchased 8/19/41. One Major E. A. Peterman took delivery for the experimental Engineering Section, Material Division, Wright Field. Substantially identical to the preceding airframe (except weighing 724 lbs.), its military Aircraft Record Card is also so inaccurate as to appear fabricated. Again, it is absolutely verifiable from other contemporary official records that it was NOT "received" on 12/8/41, and was NOT removed from flying status with only 2.8 flying hours since new, and was NOT transferred as an instructional (non-flying) airframe to the Army Air Corps Technical School at Chanute Field near Champaign, Illinois. Other records show this airframe initially "tallied off" to the Aircraft Mechanic School at the Army Air Base in Lincoln, Nebraska, and then going to the NE Nebraska Wing, CAP. After the war it returned to civilian ownership and is again on active FAA registry with its original N# 37143 designation.

With "20-20 hindsight", ERCO was the proverbial "day late and dollar short" competing for contracts Culver got. Neither manufacturer had produced in quantity in early 1941, but postwar production of the Ercoupe proved they could have produced 35 a day after nine months. In 1946, an experimental "Super Coupe" was built with retractable gear, and another Ercoupe "off the line" was fitted and tested with a 100 hp Lycoming powerplant.

While prewar and postwar Ercoupes were mostly aluminum, ERCO redesigned and built several with a plywood fuselage molded under pressure at high temperature in a form in a large tank, a center wing spar of solid laminated birch covered entirely with plywood, and outer panels of wood construction covered with fabric. By 1942 this 415-CA model was in the production certification process, but America was at war. ERCO would get government contracts to produce gun turrets instead of wooden drone aircraft, and go on to earn a number of the coveted "E" awards for wartime production goal achievements.

PUTTING IT ALL TO WORK

NOLO operations at the Santa Ana Naval Air Station in Southern CA were well supported. Two Navy blimp hangers there were the world's largest wooden structures in the world. One housed the blimps that flew patrol missions along the Pacific coast. Radio control squadron VU-7A was commanded by LCDR C.W. Bailey and operated out of one end of the other hangar with offices for the various departments including the officers section. One room was devoted to communications. A full time radio operator was on duty at all times because most radio communications at the time were by Morse code. Audio was seldom used. All messages were transcribed onto official Navy forms and delivered to the various departments. Although all aviation radiomen qualified to copy at 28 words per minute in Morse code, those assigned to working on the drones instead of a Morse code key would lose this level of proficiency. Several crew members were amateur radio "hams" off duty, and these kept the Radio operator chair manned.

Walking from the offices to the flight line, one passed the "coffee shop." For a few hours in the morning this small room had coffee and donuts available. Tended by one of the seaman, it helped keep up morale.

Next was the hydraulic shop, which maintained the hydraulic servos. Drone "commands" were radio transmissions which essentially opened or closed circuits. The opening or closing of these circuits activated or deactivated the physical force necessary to operate a drone's control surfaces, throttle, landing gear, etc. Two tough CPO brothers named Tritipo ran a "tight" shop. Not quite Mafia, but you get the idea.

Another section housed the sheet metal, woodworking and paint shop. Even though the drones were made of wood, their aluminum cowlings needed attention from time to time. Bullets holes in aluminum or wood had to be repaired. The woodworking section had special procedures to repair and treat the compressed plywood skins which covered most of the airplane. A badly shot up drone would look like it just came from the factory after it was repaired. It might come back from its next mission in even worse shape, and still be repaired to look like new again. The Navy always seemed to keep its personnel busy.

Aircraft mechanics next door mechanically maintained the drones. Because of the constant abuse suffered on missions extensive care and inspections were required to keep engines and airframes airworthy. When there was no pilot in the drone, even simple malfunctions could not be corrected in the air, so a drone that had just returned from a mission required much more than just a cursory glance.

Chief Petty Officer Frank Boaz was the keeper of the electrical shop. Stacks of batteries were on charge almost continuously and everything electrical was kept in tip-top shape.

Chief Jerry French was in charge of the radio shop. Here, crews of a dozen or more aviation radiomen kept the vacuum tube radio control systems reliably operational. To do so required many hours of checking and rechecking. Technology was continually advancing and that meant staying "on top of" all new modifications. Along the walls were shelves stacked full of test instruments, television sets, wires and cables of all sorts. Some of the technicians worked on the bench wiring cable harness plugs with 18 soldered connections. These connected the control boxes to the transmitters. As completed they were plugged into a test box where each circuit was connected to a light. If all of the lights worked you were in business. If one light failed, you had a loose connection in the plug. Everyone had a job to do, from troubleshooting radios, routine maintenance, to completing radio checks on the line.

The main challenge for everyone, of course, was to keep the 12 TD2C-drones parked outside operational.

Each day an exhaustive test routine had to confirm that each drone and its controller aircraft (JRB-1) were ready to go at a moments notice. Some of the JRBs were fitted with an expanded greenhouse and designated Expeditor, which afforded the drone control pilot increased visibility. On NOLO days they were checked twice. The first task in the morning was to place a radioman in a drone and one in the controller aircraft. The drone engine was started and radio checks conducted with visual signals from each aircraft. The vibration of the engine made it easier to find bad tubes and improperly soldered wire connections with intermittent problems.

As the controller activated each control, the correct response by the drone was confirmed by the man there. When the control box signaled up elevator the stick in the drone moved back and the elevator went up. At that point the radioman in the drone would signal the controller by tapping his head twice. This was the signal that the elevator control was working. All of the controls could be individually checked this way except the retractable landing gear. When the drone was sitting on the ground a squat switch was enabled to keep the wheels from retracting. The wheels would only retract when the aircraft was in the air. Of course, some of the ferry "safety pilots" managed to land with the wheels retracted anyway. All in all, these small aircraft were sophisticated machinery for their time and a credit to their designers. At various times, the facility could have as many as 14 TD2Cs, several JRB-1s, 6 F6F-5Ks, 0 SO3-C Seagulls and 6 F6F-2D chase planes. The choice of drones for an exercise depended upon the simulation and speed needed.

NOLO operations were flown from the Palisades. This was a small auxiliary field next to the Pacific with a paved runway 2500' long and 100 yards wide. All radio and mechanical checks were completed very early in the day before the squadron would travel in convoy from Santa Ana NAS to the Palisades.

FOX-1 occupies the ground controller's chair for a landing attempt. to recover the drone from a NOLO exercise. The observer is there as a safety back-up Photo: Victor Smith

Two aviation radio operators take a break outside of a hot radio communications truck FOX BASE, while a NOLO exercise is going on in the Pacific. There is always someone on duty inside. The aviation radiomen assigned to this truck are responsible for communications between the airplanes, monitoring the NOLO exercise, and communications with the Main Base at Santa Ana; Photo: Victor Smith

TD2C Culver Cadet Target Drone. Photograph courtesy of: National Museum of Naval Aviation

The author at Experimental Aircraft Association (EAA) convention in Oshkosh, WI 2000. TD2C drone in background donated by Morton Lester.

TD2C on runway. Photograph courtesy of: National Museum of Naval Aviation

Four drones in front of the line shack in 1943. Photograph courtesy of: National Museum of Naval Aviation

A lonely vigil – A sailor stands guard over the drones. Photo: Victor Smith.

"Hands off" as the crew releases the RD2C Culver Cadet drone for its take off run. The ground controller ill take the drone off and hand it over to a JRB-1 drone controller who will be right behind it. The controller will guide it to the NOLO practice site .Photo:Victor Smith

Annual Bar-B-Q beer party at the Palisades. Photo:Victor Smith

Later that same day (Victor is on right kneeling). Photo:Victor Smith.

Radio Shack at VU7-A, Naval Air Station, Santa Ana (1947). Photo: Victor Smith.

JRB 17/2 scale model used in Photoshop rendering Photo: Ken Kiefer

TD2C 17/2 scale model for Photoshop cover. Photo: Ken Kiefer

Culver TD2C at EAA's Oshkosh Museum. Donated by Lester Morton. Photo by the author.

Aerial view of the Naval Air Station at Santa Ana, CA. The two hangars are the largest in the world and were made to house the blimps that patrolled the pacific coast. One was assigned to Drone squadron VU7-A,. The other held the crew that operated the AVR boats.

Close-up of Blimp hangars at Santa Ana.

PQ-14 Culver Cadet target drone: Air Force Photo

JRB-1 guiding a TD2C drone outbound to prepare for a torpedo attack on the ship. The gunners aboard the ship will use live ammunition and try to destroy the drone. There are no photographs of NOLO operations. They were top secret. Photoshop rendering by Ken Kiefer.

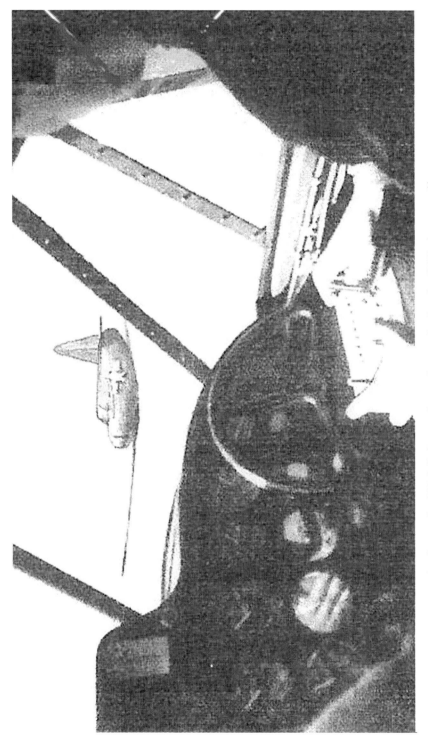

A view of a TD2C drone from the cockpit of a JRB-1 controller. Courtesy of Experimental Aircraft Association, Oshkosh, WI.

Chapter 7

PALISADES

THE NUTS AND BOLTS AT A PALISADES' 'NOLO'

Much of the following information was submitted by U.S. Navy Aviation Radioman Victor Smith. He spent 2 years in VU7-A at the Santa Ana Naval Air Station. Many of his on site photographs are included and credited.

The trip to the Palisades was not far. The convoy for a one day operation was led by a rather large radio truck, painted yellow, that towed a trailer with a 24volt DC arc welder power supply and contained all the radios necessary to communicate with the main base, pilots flying the aircraft, and the drone radios and ground control systems. From it the active NOLO frequency was monitored from the active site while a NOLO mission was in progress. A jeep followed, which was used to carry the pilots to and from the drones. When an unmanned drone overshot the runway after a mission it would otherwise be a long walk for the pilot whose job it was to taxi it back. Following the jeep would be a small fuel truck, an ambulance, and several private cars to carry the crew and some of the pilots.

Palisades was situated on the top of a rather large mesa with a direct view of the Pacific. Flying the unmanned drones from there provided a safety cushion by not having them over populated areas at any time.

When the vehicles arrived the first thing was to erect a few tents to provide some shade.

The radio truck was set up to monitor the flights from the main base. Approximately mid field, the chair for the ground control operator was set up. It would be back from the runway and elevated to give the ground control pilot the best view of the field for drone take offs and landings. The mechanics and the rest of the crew set up their temporary areas and soon the field was ready for the arrival of drones from Santa Ana.

Meanwhile, back at Santa Ana, the drones and the JRB-1 drone controllers completed all their check lists. The drones were ferried to the Palisades by safety pilots. These took off first so as to be set up on the ready line before the JRB departs. The JRBs evolved from a long line of Beech twins starting with the original Model 18 in 1937. Many design changes over the years were incorporated in the model JRB-1 Expeditor. This drone controller version had an expanded greenhouse that gave the drone control pilot the best possible view. Over 9,000 JRBs were built.

Air to air and air to ground call signs were usually "Gaywings" one or two. This was for voice communication between the incoming planes and the radio truck during the flight from Santa Ana. Now, as promised, we will continue with the story begun on page 3 of this book so you will understand what was really happening with the Cadet, i.e. the drone.

As each drone arrived, it was taxied to a tie down areas except one. That one would be for the first mission, so it would be stationed at the center of the departure end of the runway with its engine still idling. The safety pilot and ground controller would again verify all radio controls operated properly. Once the pilot turned the auto pilot on and exited, the ground controller in his chair by the runway now had sole control of the drone. The ground controller's carrier switch was on, his call sign was "Fox One" and everyone now looked for the JRB drone controller aircraft to appear and to take over the control of the drone.

As the airborne JRB comes in sight, his call sign became "Charlie One." The F6F-2D flying with the JRB for the exercise became "Charlie Two." "Charlie Two" was a "back up" controller and carried a full set of radios. Charlie One would control the drone at all times after the hand off from Fox One unless something went wrong. The only call signs used would be Fox One and Charlie One once the operation started. No deviations were allowed from that rule for safety reasons.

As the JRB approached the field, a crew of nine attended the idling drone. The crew chief would have three men stationed behind each wing and one behind each horizontal stabilizer as the drone revved up to go.

The JRB would turn into a downwind flight pattern leg, and confirm he was ready for the transfer of radio control. As Charlie One turned onto his base leg, Fox One would confirm that the ground crew was ready. As Charlie One turned onto the runway heading, the ground control pilot selected throttle control with his stepper switch and applied full power to the engine with the function switch on his right, the crew holding back the wings released them and those at the rear would hold a bit longer to correct the drone's alignment with the runway as they released their individual horizontal stabilizers.

As the drone picked up speed, Fox One would lift the drone off at approximately sixty five mph. With regular practiced orchestration, the JRB would then be just behind the drone for the transfer of drone radio control. An alert observer standing near Fox One would watch the unfolding sequence of events to assure any possible emergency was dealt with quickly and as best possible.

With the drone in the air and the controller positioned close behind, Fox One would advise, "Charlie One this is Fox One, TAKE CONTROL." On hearing this, the radioman sitting directly behind the drone controller would flip his carrier switch ON and reply "This is Charlie One WILCO, (will comply), CARRIER ON." That confirmed that the JRB now was on the carrier frequency. Fox One would reply "ROGER, CARRIER IS OFF," as he flipped his carrier switch OFF. For a few seconds the drone was receiving two carriers during the transfer of control, but better to have two than none.

The JRB now had sole control of the drone from this point until it was brought back for recovery. With the three aircraft on their way to the practice area, Fox One ground control would be monitored until Charlie One confirmed by radio that the drone was under control and would not be returning for an emergency landing. Most crew members could stand down with little to do now but wait. Voice transmissions between the ship and Charlie One during the NOLO were monitored from the communications truck.

Chapter 8

'NOLO' REVISITED

During the flight to the practice site, there was time to think about what they were doing here in the first place. Was it merely a "go through the motions" performance of the same old gunnery practice or was it to increase the experience and skill level of anti-aircraft gunners? In truth, the practice was a little of both; but there was now an entirely new urgency motivating everyone to do everything possible. A new and increasing challenge blared from Navy loudspeakers on ships in the Pacific.

'KAMIKAZE INBOUND'

In 1944 and 1945, the kamikaze exacted a terrible toll on allied shipping in the Pacific. The Japanese knew that they were losing the war. As a last resort, they hoped to turn the tide in their favor by loading aircraft with explosives and crashing it into enemy ships. Thousands signed up for Kamikaze suicide missions. Most were volunteers although there was incredible peer pressure to do so. Most Japanese believed their Emperor was a God and their pilots were eager to do anything they believed would please him.

In the first attack in 1944, the escort carrier St. Louis was sunk and thirteen other escort carriers were damaged. In 1700 attacks in 1945 they damaged their target 20 percent of the time.

Two Escort Carriers and three Destroyers were sunk, twenty-three Carriers, five Battleships, nine Cruisers, and twenty-three destroyers were damaged. A total of 738 men were killed and 1,300 wounded during the attacks. Some 5,000 Kamikaze pilots died in those attacks, but over 20,000 were still looking forward to their mission when Japan surrendered, some of which are still alive.

The most successful Kamikaze aircraft were Zero fighters. They would take off from airfields in southern Japan and navigate to the enemy fleet. A direct hit at or below the water line was preferred, although simply crashing into the superstructure with enough explosive would tear up a ship pretty badly. Another popular and effective tactic was to approach the ship from the stern, rake the deck with gunfire and then crash onto it. To eliminate the radar threat, at times there were attempts to knock out the destroyers first.

The Cherry Blossom was a small rocket powered aircraft with only a 20 mile range. It had to be carried into battle and released by a Mitsubishi "Betty" bomber before it could dive into a ship at high speed and destroy it. Once these Betty's entered the defense radius of fighter protection around carrier groups, they were sitting ducks both slow and of limited maneuverability both before and after release of their missile. The Japanese scrapped the idea after achieving little success with it.

Returning to the NOLO mission with the 3 aircraft enroute to the practice area, the drone would be in front with the JRB just below and to the left. This afforded a drone controller in the right seat the best view of the drone. The F6F flew loose formation with the JRB.

All the other aircraft needed to do was to follow the drone. Once set, the drone's 3-axis Sperry P1-K autopilot would fly it to the ship with an altitude error of only 20 feet. For its time, this was a very sophisticated aerial achievement.

As the distance to the ships closed, voice communication between the JRB controller and the ship was established. They would review prior plans for the NOLO to confirm that each plane was where it was supposed to be at any given time, and whether a run would be a strafing, bombing or torpedo attack.

Some runs were made broadside to the ship and if the ship was moving, corrections would have to be made to keep the ship aligned with the drone. At the beginning of the bomb run, the drone would be lined up to the ship and as soon as the drone was on its way, the Controller and Back-up plane would turn away for some distance and proceed to fly parallel with the drone. The directive to the gunners was: **"SHOOT ONLY AT THE RED AIRPLANE!"**

Charlie One would call the ship when they were on station and awaiting orders. A torpedo run was the first request of the day. This run would have Charlie One direct the drone toward the ship at 300 feet with the 3 axis auto pilot set to hold it on heading and on altitude (plus or minus twenty-five feet).

As the drone headed for the ship on its run, Charlie One and "Charlie Two" would veer port (left) to fly a parallel course to the target maintaining visual contact with the drone at all times. Aboard ship it was again announced:

"SHOOT ONLY AT THE RED AIRPLANE!"

A barrage of gunfire reached from the ship for the incoming drone. With so many guns firing it seemed impossible the drone could survive the run, but most of the time they did.

The drone passed over the ship and the other side had their turn as it departed outbound. Charlie One would confirm when the site was clear and line up with the drone again to start another run. As long as it was on the other side of the ship, Charlie One could switch off the autopilot and line the drone up to approach the opposite side of the ship. This gave gunners a chance to fire both coming and going. If enough time and drone fuel remained, they would service another ship. It was important to end practice with enough fuel to get the drone back to Palisades.

Leaving the ships behind the trio headed back home. Most of the time, the drone remained controllable. If some of the controls would not respond, Charlie One would have to decide if the drone could safely return Palisades or not. If the landing gear was inoperable or the throttle stuck, he could scratch the drone by diving it into the sea, or shut down the engine and let it settle and sink. While no chances were taken trying to save a potential runaway, it was seldom that a drone was shot down or ditched.

Back at Palisades, the ground crews were ready. The fire truck and the jeep were on standby. The 3 aircraft approach the field on an extended downwind leg approach. The ground controller, Fox One, would confirm he was ready to recover the drone. Charlie One would lower the landing gear and the drone was guided around the base leg and set up on final approach.

Ground control, Fox One, would be in his chair with the observer standing by as the drone approached. When Charlie One had correctly stabilized the drone's air speed and altitude, he would say, "Fox One this is Charlie One, take control." Fox One would respond with "Charlie One this is Fox One. WILCO, CARRIER ON." Charlie One would respond "ROGER, CARRIER IS OFF," as he fliped his carrier switch OFF. The transfer of control was ALWAYS done like that, with no exceptions.

Fox One now had sole control of the drone, and would reduce power so it would descend and land the drone from that point by slowly reducing the throttle and letting the drone descend toward the runway. At the proper moment he would flare and the wheels would touch down. With the function switch at step three and application of "on" function, brakes were applied. Most of the time the drone would stop somewhere on the runway and the fire truck was not needed. The recovery jeep would deliver a safety pilot to the drone to taxi it back, and park it in the inspection area.

Now the mechanics, radiomen, and the rest of the ground crew would swarm over the drone like bees, looking for something wrong to fix. Top priority was to make it sufficiently airworthy for the short flight back to Santa Ana. If this was not possible, they would leave it there and get a trailer to transport it back to base.

Controller aircraft did not land at Palisades, but continued back to Santa Ana. When the drones and the rest of the crew got back, if there was time, they might assess the damage. Most of the time they just pulled the drone into the hangar until another day.

Chapter 9

F6F Drones

Frank Dailey provided many of the following details and facts on the F6Fs, as well as personal insights and photos:

The Grumman F6F Hellcat series had its beginnings back in 1939, but did not reach the Pacific theater in significant numbers until June 1942. It evolved from the earlier F4F Wildcat but an electric landing gear replaced manual crank-up gear, the wing was mounted on the bottom of the fuselage instead of the middle, and it was bigger, faster and heavier with more armor, range and firepower. The U.S. Navy and Marine Corps used it in the fighter role to down over 5,000 enemy aircraft with a kill ratio of 19:1. The last of 7,800 F6F-5s manufactured came off the production line in November 1945.

During the last part of the war, there were lots of F6Fs on hand, and many were converted to drones with the F6F-5K designation. F6F 5-Ds and 2 F8F-D Bearcats were used as drone controllers, now called "Chase One" and "Chase Two." The D models sported yellow wing and tail surfaces.

The specifications for the F6F-5K drone were impressive.
>   Wingspan 42 ft. 10 inches.
>   Length 33 ft. 7 1nches
>   Height 13 ft. 1 inch
>   Max speed at altitude 380 mph or 330 knots
>   Service ceiling 37,300 ft.
>   Range 945 miles or 820 nautical miles

In 1944, the F6F-5K drone entered service. The weight and space required for improved radios and other electronic gear were no longer a problem. By then, the 180 mph top speed of the little wooden TD2C was far too slow to realistically simulate the Japanese fighters being used in the Kamikaze role, but the F6F-5K could hit 380 mph. When a F6F-5K headed toward a ship at up to 380 mph, the threat was clear; and every gunner instantly knew the difficulties they would have to overcome to provide their ship effective Kamikaze defense.

Franklyn E. Dailey Jr. was in the U. S. Naval Academy Class of '43, but graduated in June 1942 in the first WW II three year class. He served on the USS Edison for 27 months during which the ship was awarded 5 battle stars and commendation with combat V in the North Atlantic/Mediterranean theater, and as Gun Boss from Jan-Oct. 1944. Frank was assigned to flight training Oct. 44-May 45 and then to VP 107 Whidbey and Aleutians, for ECM patrols in PB4Y-2s. He attended Naval Post Graduate School at Annapolis, earning a Bachelor of Science degree in Electrical Engineering and UCLA 1950-51 earning a Masters degree in Applied Physics as a Lieutenant Commander, USN.

He has not only contributed interesting details of his missions, but provided photos from his book, "The Joys of Instrument Flying". The following narrative is his story:

"On arrival VX-2, NAS Chincoteague June 1951 I was assigned as Projects Officer, and controlled all OPDEVFOR projects except drones. I did fly the F6F-5K (to check them out) and the F8F as a chase pilot. Being strictly a pilot, I was not briefed on the drone 'project'.

From experience then, our NOLO flights served the USS Mississippi, BB-23. This was a 13,000 ton ship with 12 inch guns built around 1910, that underwent several conversions, the last to a project ship which would test fire the Terrier missile.

Terrier, Talos, and one other missile were designed and built by Johns Hopkins Applied Physics Laboratory in the missile development years following WW II. Terrier (the one I flew drones for) was an AA missile guided missile with an influence fuse. Likely several designs were being tested, but pilots of control plane flights were not informed on any of those matters.

We took the F6F-5K to altitudes given by Mississippi, over VHF and later UHF voice circuits. We put them on courses as directed by U.S Mississippi. There was no ground preflight briefing as to what would be undertaken on any given day.

Most often the Mississippi would take control by the usual 'my carrier is OFF' and then they would speak, 'my carrier is ON.' At the end of a firing run, Chase 1 would take control back and reposition the drone for another firing run.

The object would be to see the fuse actuate (success), or fail to actuate, (failure). I never knew how they distinguished between a fuse problem or a guidance problem (too far away to trigger the influence fuse).

On a few occasions the warhead would be fully loaded, not just a fuse with some marker smoke, but to try to down the drone. If the missile actually hit the drone, the drone would usually crash. We had drones that survived 10-15 flights and would be brought back and reused. The F6F would take a lot of punishment and would come back even with flight surfaces damaged. 'Shot up' was the usual terminology. Sometimes Chase 1 and Base would decide that a drone that was flyable was not landable and it would be ditched at sea.

Our flights were out over the Atlantic, two chase F8F chase planes, one F6F-5K drone, and the USS Mississippi involved. Main test flights for the F8F were to take it to 35,000 feet if you could get it there, and provide time for an instrument to record the Carbon Monoxide. There was a suspicion that the firewall in the F8F "leaked." The instrument configuration was a 'special' put in the cockpit just for that flight. Another feature of the plane was a manifold pressure regulator. If a pilot passed out the MPR would settle on 35 inches of Hg. If the thing malfunctioned (and they occasionally did), you had to land by cutting the magnetos in the approach to the runway. The only other problem was make sure you pulled the prop thru before starting. The master jug was on the bottom and it could load with oil and "hydraulic," leading to quick engine failure. This happened once on takeoff at Chinco, and the pilot did not survive.

It was a daily routine to test F6F-5Ks and preflight them for NOLOs. We tested all the control circuits with ground control in the vicinity of NAS Chincoteague. One of our best pilots, Eric Lichnerowicz, was killed in such a test when the drone nosed over and crashed, likely a carrier frequency failure. There was a big red handle just under the lower left instrument panel to pull. It would disengage all circuits in an emergency. Some evaluators felt that some pilots likely could not reach and engage that handle, particularly under negative g-force. I think Eric was just too close to the ground when he was running through the test. As I say, he was a far better single engine pilot than me with lots of experience, possibly too confident. The most skilled pilots had the accidents. Gordon Scrogge Wiley, class of '42 USNA, a mentor and friend of mine, walked away from a runway crash of a drone because he was willing to let Fox take him in for a landing too far before he took control. Harold Norman landed an F8F wheels up after flying too many drone missions one day and getting too tired to be alert. Also, the Chinco runway had a dip in it where the tower could

93

not see an approaching plane and whether its wheels were up or down.

The main lesson I learned was not to fly more missions on any day when I was already tired from mission flying. One of my projects was to take a P2V-2 to 25,000 feet on an ECM project flight. We used the diluter demand oxygen for the crew and the a/c staggered at that altitude. After 5-6 hours every one in the crew was tired. Many accidents were attributed to that exact scenario. All in all, the pilots as a whole had few fatal accidents. It seemed that according to statistics, most of them were pilots with high time and it is possible that they were caused by pushing the envelope a bit. Radio failures in the drones were quite rare, and relatively few were ditched during a NOLO or other training sessions."

Perhaps the best known failure occurred in a F6F5-K drone, which resulted in a rather spectacular series of events around Palmdale, CA, appropriately titled "The Battle of Palmdale."

Grumman F6F-5K drone and 2 F8F Bearcat controllers.
Photograph used by permission from Frank Dailey's book: Triumph of Instrument Flight.

A Navy F6F 5-K drone and two F6F drone controllers, chase 1 and chase 2 on a test flight Courtesy: 1952 Air Trails

.

Franklyn E. Dailey Jr, on right, when he was Commander USNR and
CO of VF-852 shown here with co pilot Ken Condra going over details
of a mission flight out of NAS Niagara Falls, NY Photo: Frank Dailey

Douglass SBD. Controller for TD2C drones.
Courtesy National Museum. of Naval Aviation

An F6F-5K of VX-2 at NAS Chincoteague, Virginia about 1952.
At least the brakes were OK. Photo: Frank Dailey Jr.

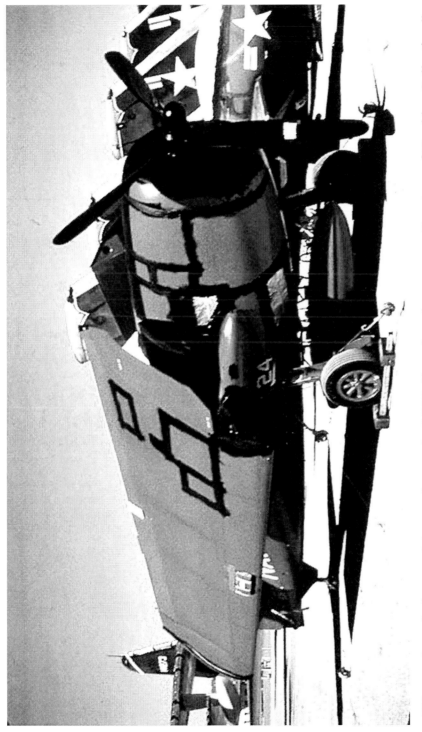

When a drone is damaged, it must be repaired F6F-5k undergoing surgery. Courtesy of "Larkins Collection."

General Motors TBM-3U in flight. Notice that the gunners turret is removed to provide a seat for the drone control pilot, DCP. The aircraft control pilot, ACP, is flying and two radiomen occupy the lower compartment. Courtesy "Larkins Collection."

One of five TBM drone controllers formerly used to control the TDR-1 drone in the Pacific, was transferred to Norfolk VA. for overhaul. They became Airtankers for the US Forest Service. Courtesy of : "Larkins

Douglass JD-1 with KD target drones attached to the wings.
Utility squadron VU0-3 at NAS Brown field, April, 1960. Courtesy of "Larkins Collection."

US Navy Grumman Bearcat drone controller.
Wings and tail are yellow and the fuselage is Navy blue. Courtesy of "Larkins Collection."

Fox 1 ground controller landing an F6F 5K drone at Palisades

An F6F-5K at Johnsville Pa. an official US Navy photograph, from the collection of John D. Voss

F7F Tigercats were used for drone controllers for the F6F-5D drones. UD-VU-4 at Dayton, Ohio in 1963. Courtesy of "Larkins Collection."

Douglass JD-1 with KD drones at Pt. Mugu in 1955 Photo by Dusty Carter. Courtesy of "Larkins Collection."

Squadron VX-2 Flight Line at Chincoteague, VA, 1951. JRB's, TD2C's, F8F Bearcat controllers and F6F-5K drones. Photograph courtesy of: Frank Dailey.

F6F-5K Drone. Photograph courtesy of: National Museum of Naval Aviation

F8F-2D Bearcat controller. Photograph courtesy of: National Museum of Naval Aviation

Flight line ready. An F8F 2-D Bearcat drone controller next to a Grumman F6F-5k.
Ready for action. National Museum of Naval Aviation.

Chapter 10

When things go wrong: Palmdale and Joseph P. Kenndy, Jr.

"THE BATTLE OF PALMDALE"

On August 16, 1956, The Navy suffered a drone public relations catastrophe. Drone take offs are made towards the ocean for safety reasons. On this NOLO a F6F 5K took off and Chase 1 accepted the carrier to assume control of the drone. When the drone failed to respond to the controller aircraft the nightmare of a runaway drone became a reality.

Initially it looked like its heading would take it out away from land to crash somewhere in the thousands of square miles of water generally ahead. Then the drone, ever so slowly, began a gradual turn to the left. This, if continued, would place it over some highly populated areas in a very short time. Two F89 Scorpion twin-jet interceptors took off from Oxnard Air Force Base with orders to shoot down the drone. Each was equipped with 52 unguided rockets in wing tip pods. These were fired in patterns (like shot from a shotgun), and the closer the target, the more likely one or more would score a hit.

Intercepting the drone over Santa Paula, they held their fire until it was over the mountains. The first and second rocket attacks both missed the drone, but succeeded in starting fires that completely burned out 150 acres near Bouquet Canyon. The third attack sent a series of rockets past the drone into the Placerita Canyon oil fields. Several oil sumps were destroyed along with 100 acres of brush. The fourth attack also missed the drone, resulted in a fire that wiped out another 350 acres of woodland near Soledad.

The jets fired all 208 of their rockets without scratching the target drone. In Palmdale, rockets exploded in the streets, shrapnel punched radiators full of holes, and punctured tires. Despite significant property damage, no one was injured.

The drone ran out of gas east of the Palmdale airport and took out a series of Southern California Edison power lines as it crashed in the desert. The Navy wound up looking like the "Gang That Couldn't Shoot Straight" in a major public relations disaster.

JOSEPH P KENNEDY JR.

Later during World War II, The Army and Navy experimented with much larger drone aircraft to deliver as much explosive as possible for as much destruction as possible. The Army used the Boeing B-17 and the Navy used the PB4Y-1.

By this time, Germany had killed 5,000 Londoners with V-1 Buzz Bombs launched from fixed sites in France. Launch sites were well camouflaged and most had escaped bombing by the Allies. The V-1 was a relatively slow winged cruise missile with a 2,000 pound warhead powered by a kerosene pulse jet. Its gyroscopic guidance was crude, but London was a big target. The Nazi V2 rocket had just become operational with the same size warhead, but arrived from the stratosphere without warning at a speed faster than sound. The V2 was a 46 foot long liquid propelled rocket hauled by a truck that could be set up and launched in little more than an hour from almost anywhere. A V3 "Supergun" was rumored near completion and capable of hitting London with a shell every 30 seconds. The Navy decided to try using drone bombers to take out important "targets of opportunity" quickly and decisively with minimum loss of Allied lives.

Joseph Kennedy, Jr. (brother of John F. Kennedy, later President of the United States) took off from London in a PB4Y (B-24) drone loaded with 20,000 pounds of high explosives in the bomb bay. The drone was accompanied by a B-17 "controller." The B-24 had a television camera installed in the nose and transmitted a TV signal from the camera to a display in the B-17. The "picture" was of the drone's instrument panel and view from its cockpit. The plan was for Kennedy and his co-pilot to arm the bombs at a designated time and bail out of the airplane for pickup by Navy Rescue. The B-17 would then guide the drone to its target, whatever it might be.

Something went wrong on Kennedy's B-24, and the plane blew up prematurely, resulting in the death of Kennedy and the co-pilot. Unfortunately, practically none of these drones destroyed their intended targets, and the entire program was dropped as soon as the unacceptable loss of life became obvious.

So, the Target drone program had both successes and failures. It did, however, certainly improve anti-aircraft gunnery just by teaching the gunners how hard it was to hit a real airplane, and the trained gunners undoubtedly contributed to the survival of many ships and men in combat.

We have now come full circle. We have delved into the past and visited almost all of the piston powered drones that made the cut. One might wonder why we stopped with piston engines drones since there have been many developments in the years since.

The reason is quite simple. The age of jets and rockets is a wondrous one with many new and exciting innovations. What the word "drones" once completely described has spawned a huge chronology and variety of "missiles." What once was "radio control" has evolved into an almost infinite selection of "guidance systems" for "delivery."

Theirs is another story!

RECOGNIZING THE PIONEERS

At the beginning of the resurrection of target drones, the designers were more intent on experimentation, and getting the agenda in order, than making plans for a mass produced drone that would solve all of the problems at once.

Many of the first aircraft selected to the program were right off the line. The criterion here was to pick one that would be capable of carrying the expected pay load. After all, radios at that time were very heavy because everything ran on vacuum tubes and very heavy transformers. Some used 30 or more tubes. The aircraft would need to be very stable so that it could fly hands off. The control pilot had enough to think about without twiddling the controls just to keep it level.

A New Standard NT-1 was first used as a drone in 1930 and the Great Lakes TG-2 as the controller. Then came the other drones, still with the main objective of improving the overall reliability of the radio gear.

Less publicized aircraft used in the project were the Glomb, a bomber and glider combined, Fleetwings XPQ-12-A, Bell P-63-E "pinball," Great Lakes SO3C Seagull, later named Seamew, Bugs, Bats, and many others. Most of these aircraft were used very little, if at all. During this time most of the test flights were required to have safety pilots on board at all times.

As time progressed, flights were made using unmanned drones, and further refinement of the control gear led to using drones for real target practice for the fleet.

Until Reginald Denny entered the picture, all drones were from our excess military aircraft, and considering the amount of time and design improvements made in that time period, these pioneer aircraft certainly deserve their place in the history of target drone aircraft.

This De Havilland DH-82A was converted to a Queen Bee for the RAF.The De Havilland Queen Bee was actually a Gypsy Moth in disguise. It sported radio controls, an automatic pilot, and was used as a gunnery target. Courtesy of "Larkins Collections"

The RAF was exploring the use of missiles back in the 1930s and eventually progressed to the development of the Queen Bee. The British were using their exceptional radio skills, as always, and fitted the Bee with pre-set commands. The radio operator had several of these programmed into the system and could choose the maneuver of his choice. As an example he could command a dive and the aircraft would comply with a pre set dive angle. The system and the radios turned out to be very reliable. This was in 1934.

In its repertoire it had pre-sets that could provide medium level bombing runs and torpedo bombing runs. The gunners were not used to shooting at real targets and in the first tests they did not do well. In 1934 the gunners shot at a series of Queen Bee float planes and never scored a hit. In 1935 there was some improvement but it proved that the gunners needed much more practice so Britain provided targets on a regular basis. A total of 420 Queen Bee target aircraft were eventually produced, most before March 1939.

Painted in USAAF livery per official Military PQ-13 photographs (N# and wheel covers excepted). Records confirm this surviving PQ-13 as one of only two purchased by the Army..Owner Mark Harden. Photo by William Bayne.

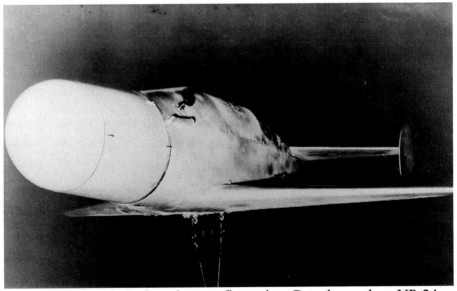

"Bat" Glide bomb. Delta wing configuration. Patrol squadron VP-24 was referred to as the "BATMEN" because this squadron did the first tests on the Bat in 1944. Courtesy: National Museum of Naval Aviation.

"Pinball"

Bell P63-A. This version was called the "Pinball" All armament was removed and the skins were replaced with Duralumin. It added 1500 pounds. Bullet proof glass was installed on all windows. A steel mesh was placed over the engine air intake and exhaust stacks. It had a thick hollow blade prop with a strobe flash in the nose cone. This would flash when it was hit, hence the name "Pinball."

The P-63-A was used to train pilots air to air combat procedures. Students would use special live ammunition that would flatten on impact and cause little or no damage. The reason for all of the special equipment was because the drone was flown with a real live pilot. It never was flown as a pilotless radio controlled drone.

A total of 232 aircraft were delivered, not exactly mass produced, but it did have an impact on air to air gunnery training.

CURTISS SO3C "SEAMEW"

The "Seamew" was intended to be the upgrade to the Curtiss SO3C Seagull. Its role as a target drone was short lived, partly because they were grossly underpowered. Some were available on floats, but could barely get off the water. A total of 250 were sent to the Royal Navy, where some nicknamed it the "Seacow." The British used them for flight training and those that were converted to drones were renamed the "Queen Seamew." It is unclear if they were ever used as target drones. Photo: Courtesy National Museum of Naval Aviation

SO3C (Seamew). Photograph courtesy of: National Museum of Naval Aviation

The Gould LBE Glob stood for glider bomb. It was towed and released, then guided by TV in a control plane. Only 4 were completed and never used operationally. The program was cancelled in Oct. 1945. Photo US Navy.

From 1930 to 1937, a New Standard NT-1 had radio controls installed and became one of the first reliable drones Courtesy: National Museum of Naval Aviation l.

Gt. Lakes TG-2 a 3 place torpedo bomber biplane converted to a drone controller. The front seat provided the drone pilot controller an excellent view. 1922-1935. Courtesy of National Museum of Naval Aviation.

An N2C-2 target drone. US Navy Project Dog. February 1939, Guantanamo, Cuba. Fleet exercises N2C-2 target drone with project personnel. Courtesy: National Museum of Naval Aviation.

Rare flying photograph of a N2C-2. Courtesy: National museum of Naval Aviation.

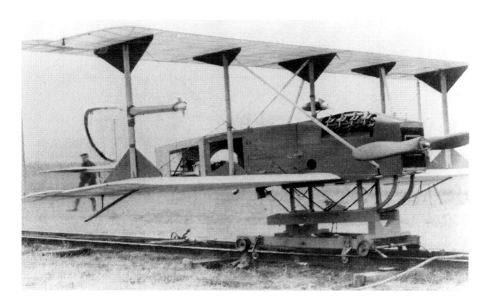

Curtiss-Sperry flying bomb, 1917-1918. One of the very first drones with an autopilot. Courtesy: National Museum of Naval Aviation.

QH-50 anti-submarine drone on the deck of destroyer USS Borie DD-704 operating in the Atlantic. 1966. Courtesy: National Museum of Naval Aviation.

Northrop BT-1 drone control plane converted from a dive bomber. Used with the Boeing FB-4 drone. Courtesy of "Larkins Collection."

Sterling Hammond JH-1 – 3 were ordered because they satisfied the air force requirements for drones. Bill Larkins shot this photo in 1930 at the San Frisco airport, painted yellow, classified Utility, with no idea what they were for. Courtesy of "Larkins Collection."

Vaught O3U-3 used on battleships and cruisers before the gear was changed from conventional to tricycle to qualify for drone specifications at that time. Courtesy of "Larkins Collection."

Boeing F4B-4 target drone usually directed by the Northrop BT-1
Probably late 1940 or 1942. Courtesy of "Larkins Collection."

The Vought O3U-6 was the tricycle landing gear version
of the O3U-3. This version was used for drone testing.
Courtesy of "Larkins Collections."

Curtiss N2C-2 modified with tricycle landing gear and flaps.
Courtesy of "Larkins Collection."

Curtiss N2C-2 Modified (8539)   *U. S. Navy*
Two radio-controlled Drones at San Diego in February. Simulated dive-bombing attack on battleship UTAH was made by one in September test.

NC2-C Tricycle gear modified . very rare photo
Courtesy of "Larkins Collection."

New Standard NT-1 radio controlled drone. 1930-1937
Courtesy of "Larkins Collection."

QF-9J. Taken at the space fair at Point Mugu.
An all red Grumman QF-9J drone.
Courtesy of "Larkins Collection."

Rare photograph of N2C2s Utility squadron VJ-1. Four aircraft showing and possibly more on the left. The Northrop BT-1 on the right is the Drone director. San Diego NAS. Courtesy of "Larkins Collection."

Foster Lane, owner and operator of Lane Airport, climbs aboard for the first flight of the brand new 2 place Culver Cadet which ultimately evolved into the TD2C drone. Photo courtesy: Clancy Hess.

Curtiss SO3C float version. Courtesy of Larkins Collection.

Conclusion

As you have noticed, this book is non-fiction in the sense that it is based on facts. Even though I was personally involved in the TD2C drone program as a young Navy AR/M 3C Petty officer, I was careful not to put myself into the story because I wanted it to be an objective, factual account of the development of RC drones. However, at the same time I did not simply want to write a reference book but instead tell the story of RC drones.

This was by no means a one man project. Throughout the past three years I have had lots of help, often from very surprising sources. One day I received an E-Mail and it read: "Hello Bill, my name is Reginald Denny Jr. I would like to help you with your book." What a beginning! Reg and his sister, Debbie McBride, provided me with much of the information about the Denny series. When Reg was just a teenager, he would sometimes accompany his father to the AVR boats and on the way home they would pass the huge hangars at the Santa Ana NAS, where at the time I was a member of the drone squadron VU7-A. Lee DiNapoli, who contributed greatly to this story was also stationed there at the same time as a drone pilot with the AVR TD. Another contributor to this book, Victor Smith. arrived at the squadron right after I left. He helped to tell the story of the day to day activities of the unit. His personal photographs are worth a thousand words, and are proudly included in the PQ-14 chapter. Franklyn Dailey, author of "The Triumph of Instrument Flying," more or less finished the drone story with the F6F-5K drones.

Except for a few personal photos sent to me, most of the photographs were sent form The Museum of Naval Aviation, Bill Larkins, and Russell Naughton. The museum was very accommodating and the Bill Larkins collection held many interesting photographs. Russell Naughton, the creator of the Hargrave website gave permission to use his material. All in all, I was very fortunate indeed.

Along with the photographs, I was also blessed with technical advice. William Bayne, good friend and aviation historian, kept me on the straight and narrow during the entire project. John Voss, also a historian, gave me lots of technical advice. Steve Hill did the formatting and prepared it for printing, and Ken Keifer designed the front and back cover.

This has been a truly unique and wonderful experience. *I move on*.

Some Fun Facts – *from my personal recollections*

Did you know?

Chase planes were equipped with live ammunition and were ordered to shoot down any drone returning from a NOLO if the controls were not responding properly in the drone. This has never been officially confirmed, but this was the talk I heard in the late 40's.

The Culver Company bid on the Culver TC2C drone for the military at a price of $2,875. The brass would not accept that amount and awarded the contract to Culver, but at a price of $3,275 per drone. The military did not think that Culver could produce the drone for the smaller amount.

NOLO operations were carried out at night. Once a month the practice exercises were carried out after dark, using only navigation lights.

By using different carrier frequencies, several NOLO operations could be carried out simultaneously.

The anti-aircraft gunners got so good that they began shooting down the expensive wooden drones at an alarming rate. The Ordinance officers aboard ships were forced to "treak" the gunsights a bit to make it more difficult to hit the target drones. I have not been able to confirm this, but again this was the scuttlebutt I often heard.

There were many young ladies working in defense plants during WWII. Of particular note for this book, there was one such lady who worked in the Dennyplane factory installing props on the TDD drones. She was noticed by David Conover, a photographer, in 1944. Because she was so pretty he took photos of her. These photos started a whole new career for the young lady, Norma Jeane. Today you would recognize her as Marilyn Monroe.